Tag Necklace

by Lea Cioci

Every grandmother carries a "brag book" with photos of the grandchildren. The Photo Tag Necklace makes your "brag book" even more accessible.

MATERIALS: 3⅛" x 6¼" shipping tag • 8½" x 11" decorative paper • Small *Magenta* floral motif stamp • Plum Wine permanent ink • Small pigment ink cubes (Pink, Purple, Blue) • Sparkle Gold pigment powder • Black *Velcro* circle • Fiber • 2 large beads • Stickers • Mop brush • Scissors • Tacky glue • Glue stick

INSTRUCTIONS: **Tag**: Ink both sides of tag by the "direct to paper" method. Lightly brush Sparkle Gold pigment powder. Stamp with Plum Wine ink. • Fold top of tag down 1" to make top flap. Fold up bottom edge of tag to this crease. • **Inside pages**: Fold decorative paper according to diagram. • Trim open edges to fit width of tag. • Glue top and bottom of folded "hot dog" booklet to inside of the tag, excluding the fold-over flap. Cut and glue photos to fit. Add stickers. • **Fibers**: Fold fibers in half. String a bead to the center point and tie knots at each end of the bead to secure. Glue fiber ends across flap crease with tacky glue so they meet in center of crease. Glue Velcro to cover hole in tag for closure. Glue second bead onto front of flap, covering hole.

Hot Dog Folding Diagrams for Tag Pages

8½"

11"

1. Fold paper in half, like this.

2. Open paper.

3. Fold paper in half.

Tag Cover Diagram

Glue Pages

1"

2½"

3⅛"

Fold

Fold

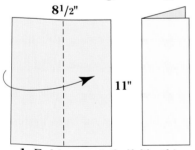

Your **paper** will look like this.

4. Fold loose ends back to meet center fold.

5. Your paper will now look like this, a wiener in a bun - a hot dog!

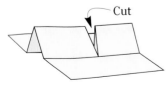

Cut

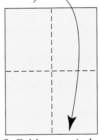

Glue pages here.

Glue photos to book pages.

Cut fold is now at bottom.

6. Cut along folded line from **the** center fold to **the** next horizontal fold.

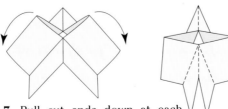

7. Pull cut ends down at each side. Your paper will look like this.

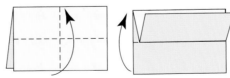

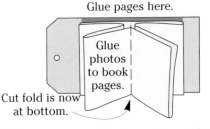

8. Turn paper upside down, this will form book pages. Glue to inside of tag.

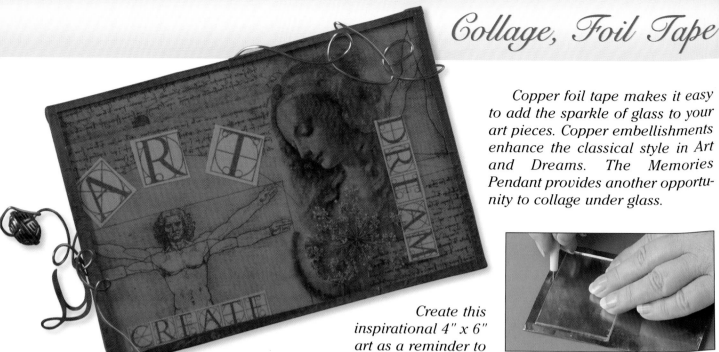

Copper foil tape makes it easy to add the sparkle of glass to your art pieces. Copper embellishments enhance the classical style in Art and Dreams. The Memories Pendant provides another opportunity to collage under glass.

Create this inspirational 4" x 6" art as a reminder to take time for yourself.

1. Trace around the glass onto Copper for backing.

Art and Dreams Encased in Glass
by Lea Cioci

MATERIALS: *Papers by Catherine* (Italian Print DaVinci) • 2 pieces of glass 4" x 6" • 24" *Venture Tape* MasterFoil Plus Copper foil tape • 4" x 6" Black cardstock • *MaVinci's Reliquary* Codex alphabet rubber stamp • *Cosmic* Copper pearlized pigment ink • Brown dye-based ink • 1 Copper bead • Metal eyelet letter "D" • Computer generated images • Dried floral • 19 gauge Copper wire • Scissors • Heat tool • Lint-free cloth • Glass cleaner • Glue Dots • Glue stick

INSTRUCTIONS: **Base:** Glue DaVinci paper to one side of Black cardstock. Collage images in a pleasing manner. See photo. Use alphabet stamps to spell out desired words: ART, CREATE, DREAM. Glue words in place. • Adhere florals with clear dots. • Collage back of Black cardstock in the same manner with fewer images. • **Glass:** Clean glass pieces, holding glass by edges. Be careful not to cut your fingers. • Sandwich collage between two pieces of glass. • **Foil:** Cut 2 Copper strips 4" long, and 2 strips 6" long. • Starting with the 6" pieces, place a strip covering ⅛" of the front piece of glass. Press from the center towards the ends to smooth and secure the strip. Fold tape over the second piece of glass. • Repeat with the other 6" strip. Apply the 4" strips in the same manner. • **Finish:** Color the metal eyelet letter "D" by tapping Copper ink onto the front of the letter and heat set. Turn over and do the same on back. • Wind wire around the upper right corner, bringing the wire to the opposite corner. Twist the wire once or twice, and string a Copper bead. Wrap wire around corner to secure. String metal eyelet letter onto the remaining wire length. Curl and twist close. Use a plate easel to display.

2. Glue collage to Copper.

3. Position image in the center of the foil tape.

Notes on Soldering

1. Soldering can be a difficult skill to master. Doing it well requires practice.
2. Purchase an iron that comes with a soldering stand and a small sponge in the base. These irons usually have a thermostat control (rheostat) in the base. The wet sponge is used to keep the tip free of dirt while soldering.
3. If you are using your soldering iron (or tip) for the first time, you need to tin the tip. Tinning is the process of heating up the iron and applying a thin coat of solder. This helps achieve maximum heat transfer.
4. Be careful when cleaning your tip. A scratched tip will lose heat too quickly.
5. Too much solder is NOT a good thing.
6. Yes, you CAN apply too much heat. An iron that is too hot will cause the solder to seep through to the other side instead of building up a bead. An iron that is not hot enough will cause solder peaks to form.
7. A good soldering job will be shiny and smooth. It will not have any dents or open spaces. A bad soldering job will look dull, more gray than silver. If the solder bead looks dry and rough, you probably kept the iron on your piece too long and cooked off the resin (or flux). If you need to redo part of your work, then re-melt and start over.
8. Re-tin the tip surface with a thin coat of solder after cleaning.
9. The iron only needs to be preheated for about 1 minute.
10. Some smoke from the resin will occur while you work. This is normal. The fumes of certain types of solder are not good for you, so solder in a well-ventilated area.
11. Store foil tape in a plastic bag to prevent oxidation. Remove oxidation with fine steel wool.
12. Wash your hands, as solder contains lead.

4. Use a bone folder to press tape to glass.

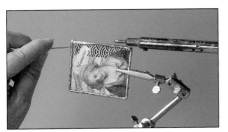

5. Apply solder.

6. Solder jump rings to piece.

7. Add beads and charm to bottom jump ring.

An iron that comes with a soldering stand makes soldering much easier.

Memories Pendant
by Babette Cox

MATERIALS: *Papers by Catherine* (Black/Gold Scallop Yuzen, Italian Print Sheet Music) • Glass 2" x 2½" • Ivory cardstock scrap • Vintage image • Computer printed word "Memories" • Jump rings (Four ¼", One ⅜") • 6 Silver 3 mm beads • Charm • *Venture Tape* ¼" wide Copper foil tape • 50" cording • Assorted beads • *AMACO* Gold Rub 'n Buff • *St. Louis Crafts Inc.* 40 gauge Copper tooling foil • 60/40 lead content rosin core thin (.032") solder • Soldering iron with rheostat or bimetal regulator • *Happ Controls* Third Hand 92-0042-00 • Bone folder (burnisher) • Newspapers to protect work surface • Glue stick

INSTRUCTIONS: Collage: On a 2" x 2½" paper, collage scallop paper, music background, "Memories" and vintage image.

Pendant: Trace around glass on Copper sheeting. Cut out slightly smaller than the glass top. Use a slight amount of glue to adhere collage to Copper. Let dry. **Assembly:** Carefully clean glass with alcohol. Do not touch underside of glass while assembling. Place the glass piece on top of collaged papers. • Copper tape has adhesive on one side, and is backed by protective paper. Remove about 5" of paper backing on foil and lay sticky side up on work surface. • Place project on its side on foil, making sure there is the same overhang on front and back. Roll glass project around while removing more paper backing and apply foil tape to the sides. Press corners, top, bottom and sides with a bone folder.

Solder: If not using solder that contains resin, paint a light coating of flux on the surface to be soldered first. See notes on soldering. • Flip work to backside. Place work on newsprint or secure it in Third Hand. Unroll about 10" of solder from the spool. • Directions for right-handed person: Hold a 4" strip of solder (from your 10" piece) with left hand. Lay across the edge of the piece. Place tip of soldering iron against foil tape to heat tape for a few seconds. Draw iron across solder in a long, slow motion right to left. (This is called beading.) Carefully remove solder first, then the iron. Doing it the other way can result in the solder being stuck to your piece. Never apply the solder directly to the iron and attempt to 'paint' it onto the metal. Practice is needed to know how much solder is enough to use to have a nice bead all along the sides. • Flip over and solder front side. Apply solder to sides. Turn image and re-clamp on each side while soldering. Solder will not stick to glass. Caution: Do not touch as solder is extremely hot. • Solder 2 jump rings ¼" from sides on top of pendant. Holding pendant in Third Hand, secure pendant with one clip and jump ring with other clip while soldering. Jump rings will be attached as pictured. Rings will appear to be sideways when looking at them from the front. Attach them so that the opening of the jump ring will be down and the split in the ring becomes a part of the soldering joint. Flip pendant upside down and solder a jump ring on the bottom.

Finish: Add 3 Silver beads, charm, and then 3 more Silver beads to larger jump ring and attach to bottom ring. Solder jump ring closed. Add Rub 'n Buff to charm and top beads. • Clean excess solder and resin residue from glass with nail polish remover. If sticky, clean with glass cleaner. Wash your hands as solder contains lead. • **Necklace:** Add beads. Thread cording through top rings.

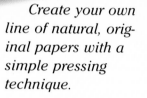

Fern Paper

by Linda Standart

MATERIALS: *Papers by Catherine* (Tiziano in various light colors; White cardstock with Silk Fibers) • Watercolor paper • Water spray bottle • Dish pan or rectangular cake pan to presoak paper • Water-based reinkers • Pressed fern fronds • 16" x 20" waterproof surface such as foam board to lay paper on • 16" x 20" sheet of glass or heavy Plexiglas • Weights for pressing (stones, bricks, pieces of cement block, heavy books) • A sunny window or a sunny outdoor spot.

INSTRUCTIONS: Prepare work surface by covering with plastic sheets, or work outside. If indoors, work over a sink.

Prepare paper: Dip watercolor paper in a pan of water, then place on a firm, waterproof surface and smooth against it. • Choose 2 - 3 colors of ink that will blend well. Pour, spray, dribble and/or brush the inks over the paper surface. Spray water to dilute areas where the ink is too dark or too concentrated or to 'push' it toward another color. Add some pearlescent or metallic accents if desired.

Leaves: Lay the pressed fronds or leaves on the paper so that there is not much left uncovered. Let some of the botanicals go off the edge of the paper. The material doesn't need to be dried, but it will be easier to manage if it is at least pressed flat. You can lightly brayer some of the plant material with a contrasting ink or with a metallic ink before laying inked side down, on the paper. The results are somewhat unpredictable, but always gorgeous. • **Press**: Cover with glass or Plexiglas and then place weights around the edge. Place in a bright, sunny window or a sunny spot outdoors. The project needs at least 8 hours exposure to sun. • **Finish**: When the paper is just damp, remove the cover and carefully lift off the ferns, leaves or other material. If you are careful, you can re-use the material for another sheet of paper. • Place between two sheets of plain paper or thin cotton cloth. Finish drying under heavy books or other weights to ensure that finished paper is flat. If the paper got too dry and buckled, you can iron it on a synthetic setting, without steam.

Create your own line of natural, original papers with a simple pressing technique.

1. Dip paper in water, place on surface, smooth down.

2. Dribble ink and move it around with a brush.

3. Next, flatten the leaves using a brayer.

4. Lay the pressed leaves on the paper.

5. Cover with glass.

6. Remove the glass. Lift ferns from paper.

7. Place fern paper between clean papers.

8. Press with an iron, do not use steam.

Handmade Fern Paper Gift Ideas

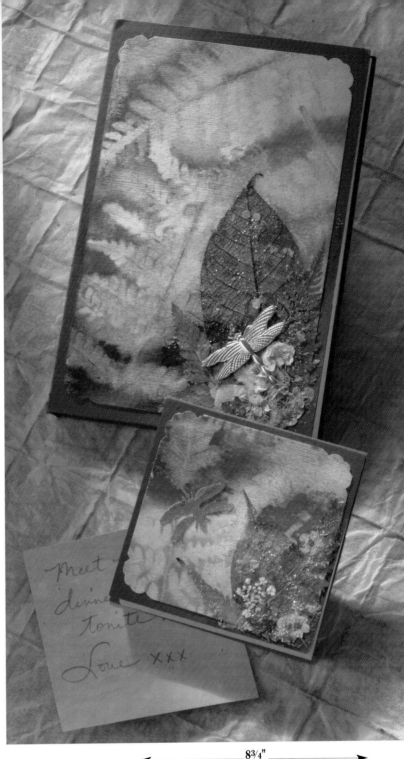

Notepad and Note Holder
by Linda Standart

Make unique gifts for everyone on your list using your own fern paper, beautiful embellishments, and coordinating cardstock. Don't forget to make one for yourself too!

MATERIALS: Handmade Fern Paper • Coordinating cardstock • 4" x 6" notepad or 3" x 3" Sticky notes notepad • Assorted embellishments • Optional Matte acrylic medium and small paintbrush for coating botanical embellishments • Ruler • Pencil • Paper cutter • Scoring tool • Heavy book or other weight • Corner punch • Tacky White glue • Glue stick

LARGE NOTEPAD INSTRUCTIONS:
Cover: Cut cardstock 8½" x 8¾". Mark cardstock according to the diagram. Score all lines. Fold 2¼" flap up. Open piece. Fold along center lines and sharpen creases. • See diagram to cut where indicated. For neat folding of finished notepad holder, remove a sliver of cardstock from cut line. • Apply a thin line of glue on the flap sides. Fold up and press into place. Let dry.

Fern paper: Cut fern paper 3¾" x 5¾". Punch corners. Glue fern paper to the front cover. Let dry under weight. Embellish as desired. Paint any botanicals with acrylic medium to seal. Set aside to dry. • **Assemble**: Fold into book. Insert notepad.

STICKY NOTEPAD INSTRUCTIONS:
Cover: Cut cardstock 3¼" x 8½". Score and fold according to diagram. Short flap on inside will hold the notepad.

Fern paper: Cut fern paper 2¾" x 3". Corner punch. Glue to cover. Let dry under book or weight. Embellish as desired. Coat any dried leaves or flowers with acrylic medium.

Finish: Place cover so you see the fern paper. Position notepad on opposite end, aligning pages with the inside fold. Glue the last page of the notepad to the flap.

Small Notepad Cover Pattern
Cut 1 Cardstock

(margin labels:) Score & Fold — Score & Fold — Score & Fold

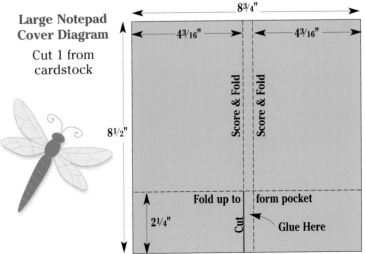

Large Notepad Cover Diagram

Cut 1 from cardstock

8¾"

4³⁄₁₆" 4³⁄₁₆"

8½"

Score & Fold

Score & Fold

Fold up to | form pocket

2¼"

Cut

Glue Here

Stamped Clay Embellishments

Sanskrit Wisdom Card

by Lea Cioci

Catch someone's attention with a stamped polymer clay embellishment and an interesting tri-fold card.

MATERIALS: *Papers by Catherine* (Indian Silk-Screen paper 5" x 8") • Red lame fabric 1¾" x 1¾" • Computer printed text • Black polymer clay • Mica powders (Green, Red, Sparkle Gold) • *Stampsmith* Arabian Nights stamp set • *Tsukineko* ink (Black StazOn, Galaxy Gold pearlized pigment) • Micro beads (Red, Gold) • *Velcro* Black circle • Small paintbrush • Acrylic roller or pasta machine • Scissors • Craft knife • *Therm O Web* (Peel n Stick laminate sheets, Super Tape double-sided adhesive and sheets) • Tacky glue

INSTRUCTIONS: **Elephant:** Condition clay. Roll out to ⅛" or run through a pasta machine on #1. Stamp elephant image in Gold into clay. Trim around elephant with craft knife. Bake following package directions. • **Sticker:** Stamp image on laminate sheet with Black StazOn. Turn sheet over and peel protective paper, exposing sticky side. Paint small amounts of mica powders onto the sticky side. Adhere double-sided adhesive sheet to the mica side of the laminate sheet. Trim around image with scissors. Remove protective backing on the double-sided adhesive sheet. Adhere to center of Red lame. • **Card:** See folding diagram. Make a tri-fold flap card with Indian paper. Adhere Red lame to the center area of open card. • Turn card over. Apply double-sided tape down each side fold. Remove protective liner and sprinkle micro beads on exposed sticky tape. Press beads into place with fingers. Turn card over. Close flaps. Adhere Velcro to elephant and to the right and left flap to secure elephant to front but enabling card to open. • Open card and tuck text inside triangle flaps.

Card Folding Diagram

Requires 5" x 8" paper.

1. Fold paper in half, like this.

2. Fold into 3 equal segments.

3. Fold corners as shown.

4. Your paper will look like this.

5. Fold flaps toward center to create a square.

Card shown actual size, 2¾" square.

Collage Cards made with CDs!

CD Love and Happiness Good Luck Cards

by ToniAnn "TA" Carbone

Etched CDs make an exciting new canvas for art. These Asian cards feature knotted cords, gorgeous papers and a stamped cut-out turned into a 3-D effect.

MATERIALS: *Papers by Catherine* (Gold/ Purple Yuzen) • Cardstock (Black, Navy, White)• CD • Stickers • *American Traditional Stencil* brass stencil • Markers or colored pencils • *New Stamps On The Block* rubber stamp • Black ink • Scissors • Sharp pointed T-pin • Awl or small electric drill • Ruler • Craft knife • *Craf-T* Decorating Chalk • 3 pieces *Mizuhiki* cord 36" long • Double-sided foam mounting tape • Double-sided tape • Tacky White glue • Stickers

GENERAL INSTRUCTIONS: **Lady**: Stamp Asian Lady image with Black ink 3 times on White cardstock. Color images. Cut all 3 images out and stack, using double-sided foam tape to attach one to the next, for 3-D effect. Tape lady to CD card as shown in the photo.

CD: Tape stencil on left side. Use a T-pin, electric drill, or awl to etch the stencil outline into the plastic. Remove stencil and tape from CD. Fill in the area of outline with etching.

Knot: Using 3 mizuhiki cords, make a knot. Tighten the ends. Tape down the ends of the knot on a piece of scrap cardstock so it lays flat. Apply glue to knot. Let dry. Cut off taped ends, turn the knot over, and tape to the CD with the points of the knot facing upwards.

Love Card: Cut Navy cardstock 6½" x 10". Fold in half (5" x 6½"). Cut Yuzen Washi paper 4¾" x 6¼". Adhere to card. • Cut CD in half. Etch. Add stickers. Adhere to card.

Happiness Card: Cut Black cardstock 5½" x 11". Fold it in half (5½" x 5½").Cut a circle 5⅜" in diameter from Yuzen Washi paper. Adhere paper to card. Adhere CD to the middle of the paper. • Add sticker borders around the edge of the CD and border of card. Add small circle of decorated paper to cover circle in middle of CD.

Love Knot

Good Luck Knot

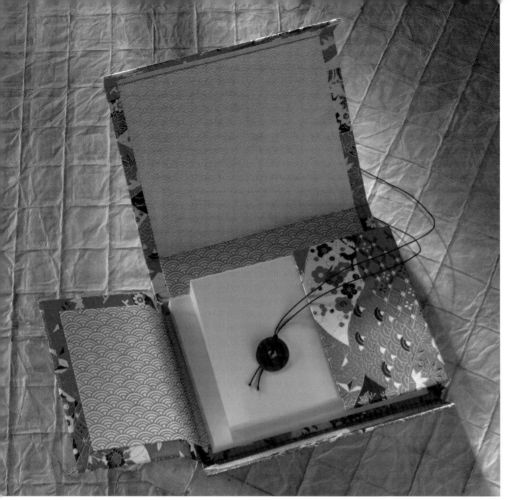

Make a useful gift from beautiful Japanese papers.

Portfolio Diagrams
Outer Boards

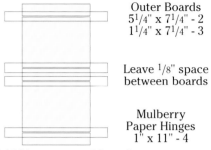

Outer Boards
$5\frac{1}{4}$" x $7\frac{1}{4}$" - 2
$1\frac{1}{4}$" x $7\frac{1}{4}$" - 3

Leave $1/8$" space between boards

Mulberry Paper Hinges
1" x 11" - 4

Fold hinges around boards and glue down.

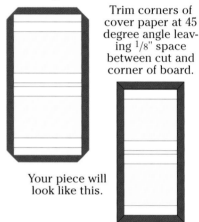

Trim corners of cover paper at 45 degree angle leaving $1/8$" space between cut and corner of board.

Your piece will look like this.

Inner Boards

Inner Boards
$5\frac{1}{8}$" x $7\frac{1}{8}$" - 1
$5\frac{1}{8}$" x $1\frac{1}{8}$" - 2
$5\frac{1}{8}$" x $3\frac{1}{8}$" - 2

Mulberry Paper Hinges
1" x $8\frac{1}{2}$" - 4

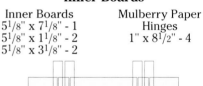

Leave $1/8$" space between boards

Fold hinges around boards and glue down.

Finish Assembly

Glue inner piece to outer piece.

- - - - - - - - -
= Folds

Outer

Inner

Lark's Head Knot

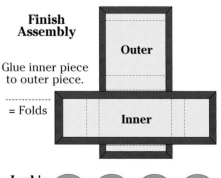

Asian Stationery Portfolio
by Catherine Mace

MATERIALS: *Papers by Catherine* (4 Stationery Portfolio book boards, 3 book boards $3\frac{1}{4}$" x $5\frac{1}{4}$"; Green/Red/Black Yuzen 24" x 36", White/Gold Scallop 24" x 36"; White Mulberry paper $8\frac{1}{2}$" x 11") • 24" Black Elastic cord • Asian coin • Bone folder • Ruler • Scissors • Craft knife • Pencil • Glue stick or spray adhesive

INSTRUCTIONS: Cutting: Outer Boards: Use 2 Portfolio boards $5\frac{1}{4}$" x $7\frac{1}{4}$". Cut 1 Portfolio board into 3 pieces $1\frac{1}{4}$" x $7\frac{1}{4}$". • Cut Red Yuzen outer cover papers $9\frac{1}{4}$" x $16\frac{1}{4}$" and 7" x 18". Cut 4 Mulberry paper hinges 1" x 11". • **Inner Boards:** Cut 1 Portfolio board $5\frac{1}{8}$" x $7\frac{1}{8}$". Cut 1 book board in 2 pieces $1\frac{1}{8}$" x $5\frac{1}{8}$". Trim 2 book boards to $3\frac{1}{8}$" x $5\frac{1}{8}$". • Cut Scallop Yuzen $6\frac{1}{2}$" x $13\frac{3}{4}$" and $4\frac{1}{4}$" x 15". Cut 4 Mulberry paper hinges 1 x $8\frac{1}{2}$". • **Hinge Assembly**: See diagrams. Glue mulberry paper to boards. Fold overhanging ends around boards. • **Outer Paper**: Cover boards with Red Yuzen. Use generous glue or spray adhesive. Turn assembly over. Smooth out air bubbles with the flat side of bone folder. Don't rub with fingers. • See corner diagram. Trim corners of cover paper at 45° angle leaving $1/8$" space between cut and corner of board. Fold overlapping paper around boards and glue down. Working from center out, use the wide end of a bone folder to push paper into spaces between boards. Use gentle pressure so paper is not torn. • **Inner Paper**: Dry fit Scallop paper on assembled boards. Working from the center out, use wide end of a bone folder to push paper into spaces between boards. Turn paper over and coat with adhesive. Re-position on board assembly aligning marks made by bone folder with the spaces between the boards. Working from the center out, smooth the paper with the flat side of the bone folder and use the wide end to push paper into the spaces. • **Finish**: See Finish Assembly diagram. Glue inner piece to outer piece. • Fold inner flaps of portfolio in and close outer cover. • Tie ends of elastic cord together, loop through coin with Lark's Head Knot. See diagram. Wrap elastic cord around closed portfolio as in photo.

Paper Collage on Glass

Madam Butterfly Collage Plate

by Lea Cioci

Go from boring to magnificent in four easy steps! You can change a clear glass plate or bottle into an art treasure in an afternoon... and it's fun!

MATERIALS: Glass plate • *Papers by Catherine* (Gold cardstock; Indian Silk-screen papers Gold/Red Ivy Vines, Gold/Black Ivy Vines) • Butterfly charms • Asian woman image • *Plaid* Dimensional Magic lacquer • *Tsukineko Brilliance* pigment ink (Galaxy Gold, Ivy) • Fibers twice the circumference of the plate • Dimensional butterfly charms • Foam brush • Tacky glue

INSTRUCTIONS: **Papers**: Tear Asian woman image. Ink the edges with Gold. Swipe Gold ink over various parts of image for subtle shimmer effect. Barely brush Ivy ink on one edge. • Brush lacquer over image. • **Plate**: Center lacquered image on the back of the plate. Smooth image from center out to form a good seal to plate surface. • Tear papers and lightly swipe with Ivy ink. Apply lacquer. Adhere to plate. Let dry for several hours. • Use tacky glue to adhere the fibers around the edge of plate and add butterfly accents.

Lotus Bottle

by Lea Cioci

MATERIALS: Glass bottle with cork • *Papers by Catherine* (Gold cardstock; Indian Silk-screen prints Gold/Red Ivy Vines, Gold/Black Ivy Vines) • Asian woman collage image • *Plaid* Ruby Red stained glass paint • Black gloss paint • *Tsukineko Brilliance* pigment ink (Ice Blue, Galaxy Gold) • Decoupage medium • 12" Gold 19 gauge wire • Accent bead • Fan charm • Foam brush • Flat, soft brush • Heat tool • Adhesive dots.

INSTRUCTIONS: **Paint**: Paint 2 coats of Ruby Red stained glass paint onto bottle, allowing each coat to dry in between. • Paint cork Black. • **Collage**: Tear papers and adhere to the bottle with decoupage medium, pressing paper from the center to all edges to remove air bubbles and make a good seal to glass. • Tear around Asian woman image. Lightly tap Gold ink around edges and slightly over background of image. Adhere image with decoupage medium. • Cut a small strip of Gold paper and adhere around neck of bottle. • **Fan**: Tap Ice Blue ink onto fan charm and heat set for at least 1 minute. Adhere fan with adhesive dot. • **Wire**: Wrap wire from front to back of bottle and crisscross the wire so that one end is shorter than the other. Bring ends back to the front. On the shorter end, twist wire in a curl and thread accent bead on and twist end over and around bead to secure. Attach to bottle with adhesive dot. Bend and curl long length of wire on the other side in a pleasing fashion.

1. Ink torn edges with Gold. **2.** Brush on lacquer. **3.** Smooth onto the back of the plate. **4.** Add collage papers.

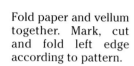

Fold paper and vellum together. Mark, cut and fold left edge according to pattern.

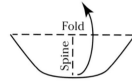

Fold
Spine

Your card will look like this.

Hearts Card Pattern

Fold

Cut

Spine Fold

Cut

Fold

Fold

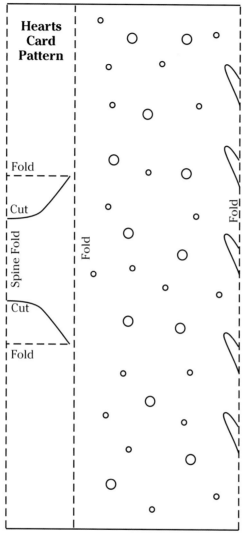

Tree Card Pattern

Cut

Cut

Fold

Spine Fold

Fold

Fold

Fold

Fold

Cut

Cut

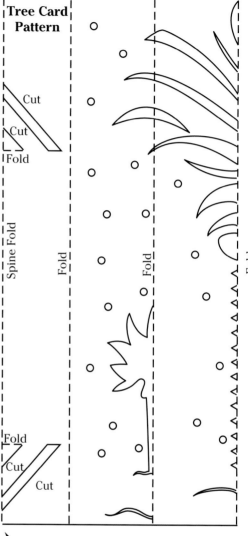

Tip: Draw pattern onto card inside pattern lines because you will cut away all lines from the transfer paper; otherwise, they will show on the front of the card.

Fold

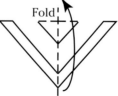

Fold paper and vellum together. Mark, cut and fold left edge according to pattern.

Your card will look like this.

1. Layer Black paper, White carbon paper and pattern.

2. Cut designs.

3. Refold and cut out more designs.

4. Fold the left edge cuts together.

with Colored Vellum

Papercutting Cards

by Sheila Cunningham

Create stunning patterns by simply cutting on folds. The designs show through beautifully when backed with colored vellum.

MATERIALS: 5½" x 8½" Black lightweight paper and colored vellum • White carbon paper • Ruler • Scoring tool • Scissors • Hole punches

INSTRUCTIONS: Fold Black paper in half 4½" x 5½". See fold diagram. Mark pattern onto middle fold and cut. Refold to create accordion folds from left edge. Line up the two fourth folds together, mark and cut. • Fold vellum to fit inside Black folded card. With both cards together, mark, cut and fold left edge according to pattern.

Fold paper and vellum together. Mark, cut and fold left edge according to pattern.

Your card will look like this.

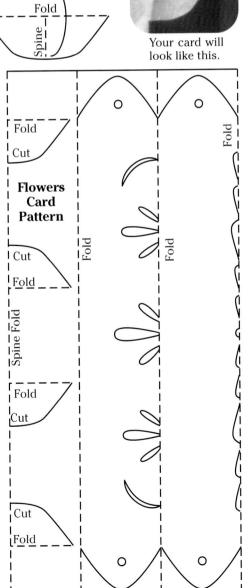

Flowers Card Pattern

Small Tag Box Pattern
Make 4

Tag Boxes

by Beverly Montez

It is so easy to make gift boxes using 4 tags and a ribbon. You will really enjoy this beginner level project. It is a great one to do with children. It's so quick, you can assemble several at once.

GENERAL MATERIALS: 20" Gold ribbon • Brayer • Embossing stylus • Hole punch • Scissors • Glue stick

For White Box: (4) 8½" x 4⅛" manila tags • 2 sheets *Papers by Catherine* Yuzen Washi (White/Gold Japanese Characters)

For Red Box: (4) 3⅛" x 6¼" manila tags • 2 sheets *Papers by Catherine* Yuzen Washi (Red/Gold Chrysanthemum)

INSTRUCTIONS: **Tags**: Cover each tag with Yuzen paper. Use glue generously and brayer over the paper to insure good adhesion. Let dry. • Use hole punch to re-punch holes on tags. • **Box**: See diagram. Layer tags, decorated side down, to form an "X". Glue the ends each on top of the other. A square will form in the center. • Score around the square. Referring to diagrams, measure out from the square on each tag and score. Fold toward the center on the scored lines, forming the sides of the box. • **Closure**: Thread ribbon up through hole of bottom tag. Pull ribbon halfway through. Thread both loose ends through hole of opposite tag and continue with remaining two tags, always pulling both loose ends through the hole. Tie ribbon in a bow on top to secure the box. Add a gift tag if desired. Trim ends of ribbon.

Tag Box Assembly Diagram for Large and Small Boxes

Fold

Large Tag Box Diagram
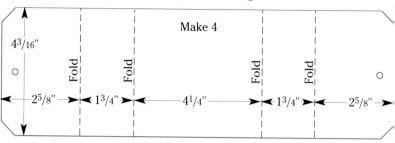
Make 4

Photo Pin Frame Pattern
Cut 1 from Cardstock

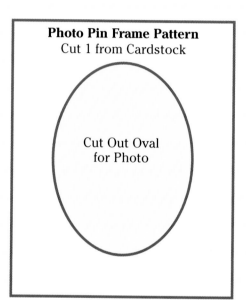
Cut Out Oval for Photo

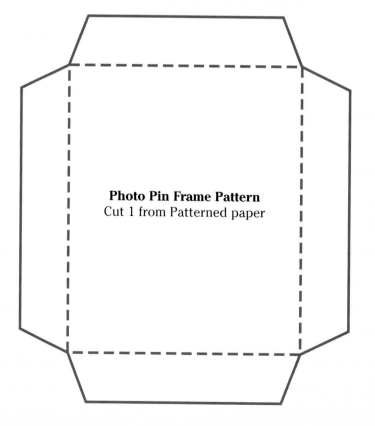

Photo Pin Frame Pattern
Cut 1 from Patterned paper

Photo Pin
by Edie Hedman

Next time you have a class reunion, make this photo pin with a graduation shot of yourself. It will be so much fun to show to all your friends!

MATERIALS: *Papers by Catherine* (Indian Silk-screened paper, Black Tiziano) • Scrap cardstock • Clear acetate • Black shrink plastic • Fine grit sandpaper • Craft knife • Self-adhesive pin back • Tape • Tacky White glue • Glue stick
INSTRUCTIONS: **Frame**: Cut Indian paper 3½" x 4". Cut cardstock 2⅜" x 2⅞" and trace frame pattern. With drawn oval side up, adhere cardstock to the wrong side of the Diamond paper with glue stick. Let dry. • Cut out oval. Miter corners. Fold excess paper to back of frame. Trim away any paper that shows through oval. Glue paper to back of frame. Set aside. • **Backing**: Cut Tiziano paper 3½" x 4". Score ½" from all sides. Fold in, making a sharp crease. Trim corners so flaps fold over easily. Adhere flaps down with glue stick. • **Photo**: Cut acetate and photo to fit behind oval opening. Tape acetate and photo to back of frame. Glue frame to backing. • **Finish**: Cut Black shrink plastic to fit backing. Sand lightly. Wipe clean. Coat sanded side with tacky glue. Lay in place on the back of the pin to get glue on both pieces. Take them apart. Let set 30 minutes until tacky. Stick together for a permanent bond. Let dry. • Sand the center of the plastic. Wipe clean. Adhere pin back to sanded area.

Pin shown actual size, 2³/4" x 3.

Here's a fabulous way to wrap those special gifts...
Tag Boxes

Book Binding Made Easy!

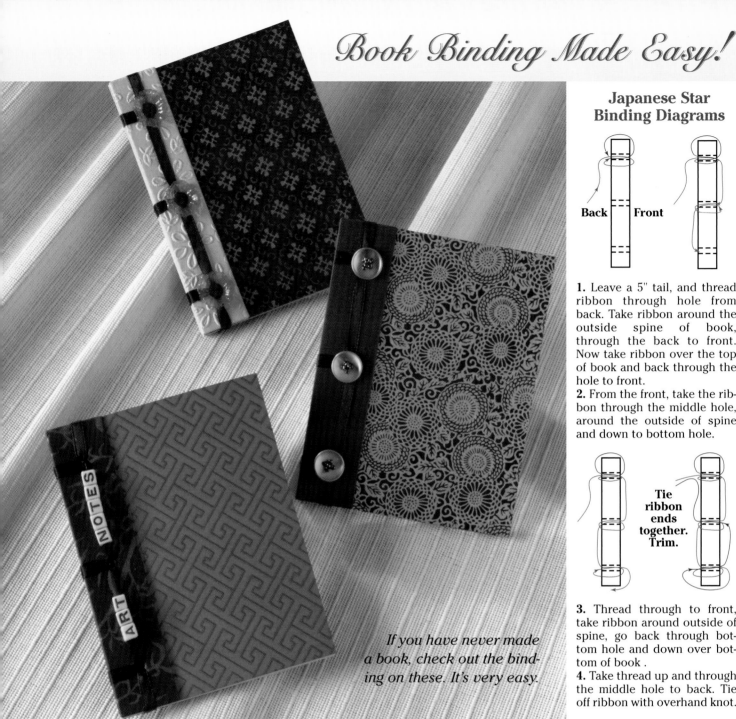

Japanese Star Binding Diagrams

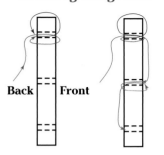

Back   **Front**

1. Leave a 5" tail, and thread ribbon through hole from back. Take ribbon around the outside spine of book, through the back to front. Now take ribbon over the top of book and back through the hole to front.
2. From the front, take the ribbon through the middle hole, around the outside of spine and down to bottom hole.

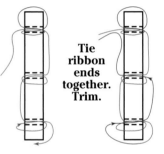

Tie ribbon ends together. Trim.

3. Thread through to front, take ribbon around outside of spine, go back through bottom hole and down over bottom of book .
4. Take thread up and through the middle hole to back. Tie off ribbon with overhand knot.

If you have never made a book, check out the binding on these. It's very easy.

Contemporary Japanese Star Binding

by Sheila Cunningham

MATERIALS: *Papers by Catherine* (Black/Gold Chrysanthemum Yuzen, Indian Silk-screen prints, Indian Embossed floral paper) • Black cardstock • Black matboard • 50 sheets 4¼" x 5½" text weight paper • 28" Black ribbon • *Art Notes* alpha beads • 3 *JHB International* Orange flower buttons with shank #705 • 3 *La Mode* Gold disc buttons with holes style 2629 • Seed beads • Thread • Needle • Hole punch • Glue stick.
INSTRUCTIONS: **Covers:** Cut 2 decorative papers and 2 Black pieces of cardstock 4¼" x 5½". Glue papers to cardstock.
Book boards: Cut 2 matboards 1⅛" x 5½". Cut 2 decorative papers

2½" x 7". Cover matboards with paper. • **Pages**: Cut 50 sheets of text weight paper 4¼" x 5½". • **Assembly**: Punch 3 evenly spaced holes in the matboard. Place matboard on each cover. Mark hole placement Punch holes. Use cover to mark holes in text paper. Punch holes. • Sandwich book board, cover, pages, cover, and book board. • Binding Follow binding directions. See the project instructions for decorating bindings.

General binding directions: Top hole: Leaving a 5" tail, thread ribbon through the hole, from the back to the front of the book. From the front, take the ribbon to the left around the spine, entering the top hole from the back to the front. Then take the ribbon up over the top of the book, through the hole again, from the back to the front. • **Middle hole**: Go through the hole from the front to the back. Take the ribbon around the spine into the hole again, going from the front to the back • **Bottom hole**: From the back, come up through to the front of the book. From the front, take the ribbon to the left around the spine

Unique Paper Bookmarks

by Sheila Cunningham

Flower Bookmark

Make elegant bookmarks with beautiful papers. This simple to make project unfolds to reveal a message.

MATERIALS: *Papers by Catherine* (Indian Embossed floral paper, Indian Silkscreen print, Metallic Gold Vellum) • *JHB International* Orange flower button with shank #705 • Eyelet • Black ribbon

INSTRUCTIONS: Print phrase to fit on 1" x 3" vellum. Cut out phrase. • Cut Black paper 1½" x 9½". Fold 4¼" from the end. Adhere vellum inside near fold. • Cut embossed paper 1½" x 1½". Align with end opposite fold. Attach with eyelet. • Push button shank through eyelet. Thread ribbon through shank and tie a knot. Tuck short end of black paper under the embossed paper.

Golden Flowers Bookmark

MATERIALS: *Papers by Catherine* (Gold cardstock, Italian Florentine print, Metallic Gold Vellum) • Gold Eyelet • Gold fiber • Glue stick

INSTRUCTIONS: Print phrase to fit on 1" x 3" vellum. Cut out phrase. • Cut Gold cardstock 1½" x 13". Cut Red Florentine paper 1" x 12½". Glue to Gold side. Fold 4¼" from one end. Fold the other end down 1½". Set eyelet in center of 1½" piece. Add fiber. • Adhere vellum inside. • Tuck the short end of the bookmark under the 1½" flap, like a match book.

Asian Fish Bookmark

MATERIALS: *Papers by Catherine* (Italian print Chinese Alphabet, Metallic Gold Vellum) • Black cardstock • Red Eyelet • Black fiber • Glue stick

INSTRUCTIONS: Print phrase to fit on 1" x 3" vellum. Cut out phrase. • Cut Black cardstock 1½" x 13". Fold 4¼" from the end. Adhere vellum inside near fold. • Cut Alphabet paper 1⅜" x 4⅛". Glue in place. • Cut fish paper 1⅜" x 1⅜". Align with end opposite fold. Attach with eyelet. Thread fiber through eyelet. • Tuck short end of bookmark under the fish paper.

entering the bottom hole from the back to the front. Go down around the bottom of the book and come up into the hole to the front.• **Return**: Go through the middle hole from the front to the back. Tie the two ends of the ribbon together on the back.

ART NOTES BOOK: Add letter beads as you go from the top hole to the middle hole on the front, threading ribbon through beads starting with the end of the word (s-e-t-o-n). When leaving the bottom hole from the front of book to the middle hole, add beads (a-r-t).

FLOWERS BOOK: At each hole, thread the ribbon through shank of an orange flower button.

GOLD DISCS BOOK: Insert thread into one of the button holes, leaving a tail of several inches. Add four or five seed beads. Exit diagonal hole. Repeat for the other two holes leaving a tail of several inches. Knot two tails together. Thread the two tails through a hole in the spine catching the ribbon and knot in back of book. Repeat with the other two buttons.

Embroidered Heart Box

MATERIALS: Paper mache heart box 5" x 6" • Scrap cardstock • Hat or floral pin • Embroidery needle • Machine embroidery thread (Red variegated, Blue/Silver variegated, Black) • Large Silver floral border stickers • 58 White flat cushion beads with center hole • Gray craft felt • Scissors • Tape measure • Black acrylic craft paint • Small foam brush • Pencil • Tape • White glue

INSTRUCTIONS: **Box**: Paint box and lid, inside and out, with 2 coats of Black. • **Pattern**: Transfer "Star in My Heart" pattern, on page 22, to cardstock. • **Piercing**: Tape pattern to lid of heart box. • Holes in the center of each heart and holes that form the small circle in the center of the design need to be slightly larger than other holes because the needle and thread will pass through several times. Pierce through pattern and box lid. • **Stitching**: Thread a needle with 24" Red thread, folded in half. Do not knot. Starting on underside of lid bring needle through hole at top center of heart, leaving 4" tail underneath. Push needle down into hole in center of heart and up again through hole to right of top center hole, then back through center hole again. Now pull thread through hole at left of top center hole • The next stitch will repeat the first stitch, drawing thread through hole immediately to the right of the first, and back through the center, and then to the left again. • Keep repeating, going through center hole at the end of each stitch, and alternating sides of the heart. Pull thread snugly on each stitch and complete stitching on the heart. • Repeat this process on the star with Blue/Silver thread, always ending each stitch by going through one of the holes that corresponds to that point of the star. There are 8 points to the star and 8 dots to the center circle of the design. • Work loose ends of thread into sewing on wrong side, add drop of glue to secure. • **Lid**: Punch 58 holes evenly spaced around edge of lid. Use machine thread to sew on cushion beads, bringing needle up through hole, through bead hole, and back through the same hole, repeating all around. Add a drop of White glue under each bead to help hold it in place. • **Felt**: Trace around box bottom and lid on felt with pencil. Cut out just inside pencil line. Glue to box bottom and inside of lid. • Measure distance around inside of upright part of lid and interior of box. Cut a piece of felt this length and same height as the box and lid. Dry-fit felt liner to check size before applying glue. Glue to inside walls of box and lid. Let dry completely before adding lid.

Paper Embroidery

by ToniAnn "TA" Carbone

In the Wind

MATERIALS: *Papers by Catherine* (Honey Gold Tiziano, Green Metallic) • White cardstock • Foam mat or old mouse pad • Hat or floral pin • Small-eye embroidery needle • Machine embroidery thread (Blue, Variegated Blue) • Corner punch • Scissors • Tape measure • Pencil • Glue stick • White glue

INSTRUCTIONS: **Card**: Cut Tiziano paper 4¾" x 9½". Fold into a 4¾" square. Round all corners. Cut Green Metallic 4⅜" square. Punch corners. Glue to card. • Cut White cardstock 3½" x 3½". Punch corners. • Copy "In The Wind" pattern, on page 22, and position onto White cardstock. Place on mat. Pierce design into cardstock. • **Stitching**: See stitching diagram. • **Center Wing**: Thread a needle with 24" Blue thread, folded in half. Do not knot. Starting with the lower center B1, bring the needle up through that hole, leaving 3" tail underneath. Push needle down into hole C25. Bring needle up through hole C24, then down through B2. Come up through B3, down through C23, up through C22, down through B4, up through B5, down through C21, up through C20, down through B6, up through B7, down through C19. Continue until center wing is complete. Work loose ends of thread into sewing on wrong side. Add drop of glue to secure. • **Left Wing**: Thread a needle with 24" variegated thread, folded in half. Do not knot. Starting with the lower left side A1, bring the needle up, leaving a 3" tail underneath. Push needle down into hole E1. Bring needle up through hole E2, then down through A2. Come up through A3, down through E3, up through E4, down through A4, up through A5, down through E5, up through E6, down through A6, up through A7, down through E7. Continue until left wing is complete. Work loose ends of thread into sewing on wrong side, add drop of glue to secure. • **Right Wing**: Thread a needle with 24" variegated thread, folded in half. Do not knot. Bring the needle up through D1, leaving 3" tail underneath. Push needle down into hole F1. Bring needle up through hole F2, then down through D2, up through D3, down through F3, up through F4, down through D4, up through D5, down through F5, up through F6, down through D6, up through D7, down through F7. Continue until right wing is complete. Work loose ends of thread into sewing on wrong side, add drop of glue to secure. • Adhere stitched design to card.

Flowers

MATERIALS: Cardstock (Plum, White, Lavender) • *Stampendous* Class-A-Peels sticker • Foam mat or old mouse pad • Hat or floral pin • Small-eye embroidery needle • Machine embroidery thread (Green, Pink, Lavender) • Corner punch • Scissors • Pencil • Tape • Glue stick

INSTRUCTIONS: **Card**: Cut Plum cardstock 5½" x 8½". Fold in half (4¼" x 5½"). Cut White mat 3¼" x 4½". Glue to card. Cut Lavender cardstock 2¾" x 4". • **Pattern**: Transfer "Flower" pattern, on page

Just For You

String art patterns in beautiful variegated and metallic threads add a unique touch to cards and other projects. You'll love making these designs with simple stitching.

MATERIALS: Cardstock (Red, Manila, Peach, White) • *Stampendous* Class-A-Peels "Just for You" stickers • Corner Punch • *DMC* variegated floss (Red, Pink) • Scissors • Needle • Foam mat or old mouse pad • Double-sided tape • Scotch tape

INSTRUCTIONS: **Card**: Cut Red cardstock 4¾" x 9½". Score and fold in half (4¾" x 4¾"). Cut Manila cardstock 4⅜" x 4⅜". Cut Peach cardstock 4" x 4". Cut White cardstock 3½" x 3½". Corner punch all pieces. • Tape Manila and Peach to card. • **Pattern**: Place pattern, on page 22, on top of the White square. Pierce holes on cardstock. • **Stitching**: Stitch with Red thread. Tape thread tail to back of card. See stitching instructions for Embroidered Heart Box on p. 20. • **Finish**: Adhere stitched piece to card. Apply stickers.

1. Place pattern on top of cardstock and mouse pad.

2. Pierce holes.

22, to Lavender cardstock. Place on foam mat or mouse pad and pierce designs through paper with needle or floral pin. • **Stitching**: Straight stitch leaves and stems with 2 strands of Green. Stitch flowers starting from the center, out to a point, returning to the center. Continue around in a circle until all points for the flower are complete. Move to the next flower. Tape thread ends to the back of the paper. • **Finish**: Corner punch stitched paper. Glue to card.

3. Stitch.

Embroidered Cards continued on page 20

Beaded, Embroidered and Folded Cards Too!

by Lin Stanley

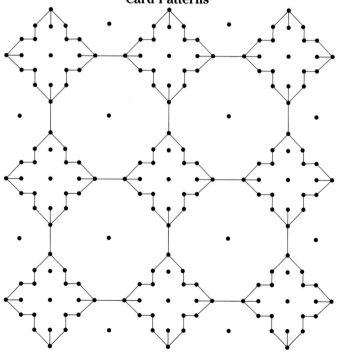

**Lavender Beadwork and
Black and Ivory Geometric
Card Patterns**

Lavender Beadwork Card

If you have been looking for a project that is relaxing to do, try an embroidered project. After piercing the holes, sit down and enjoy sewing on paper. The results are exquisite, especially when you add the sparkle of beads.

MATERIALS: Cardstock (Cream, Lavender) • *The Beadery* (9-1267A Frosted Crystal Flower Assortment, 9-880A Lavender Baby Breath Flower) • 21 Pearl seed beads • White embroidery thread • 3 *Stickopotamus* (Lavender dragonfly stickers, Gold stickers) • Beading needle • Piercing tool • Paper clips • Tape • Glue stick

INSTRUCTIONS: **Card**: Cut Cream cardstock 5½" x 8½". Fold in half (4¼" x 5½"). Cut Lavender cardstock 3¾" x 3¾". • **Embroidery**: Attach copy of pattern to Lavender cardstock with paper clips. Pierce each dot of pattern through pattern and Lavender cardstock. Remove pattern. Using White thread, stitch the first motif. Add Frosted Crystal bead, Lavender baby breath bead and Pearl seed bead in center of motif. Add Pearl seed bead to the left. • Continue this pattern until completed. • **Finish**: Glue Lavender panel with beadwork to front of White card. Add Gold and Lavender dragonfly stickers.

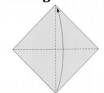

1. Fold 2" square in half unfold.

2. Fold in half.

3. Fold triangle in half, unfold.

4. Fold top triangle point down to bottom fold of triangle.

5. Fold upper folded edges (created in previous step) down, at center crease line. Make 4 of each color.

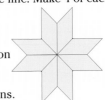

6. Position folds to make 2 medallions.

7. Layer medallions, placing top medallion diagonal to bottom medallion.

Pink Pinwheel Card

MATERIALS: *Papers by Catherine* (Plum Metallic, Italian print Fleur des Lis, Cream Tiziano, Pink Tiziano) • Cardstock • *Impression Obsession* Tea bag Folding Stamp H4470 • *Tsukineko* Encore Burgundy Metallic Ink • Punches (Large chevron, small flower, large flower) • *Stampendous* Class-A-Peels Translucent frosted stickers • Double-sided tape • White glue • Glue stick

INSTRUCTIONS: **Card:** Cut Plum Metallic 5½" x 11½". Fold card in half (5½" x 5¾"). Cut Fleur des Lis 5¼" x 5½" and tape to card. Cut another Plum Metallic 4¼" x 4¼". Tape to the center of the card. • **Quilt pieces:** Cut Cream Tiziano 4" x 4". Punch 4 chevrons out of Pink Tiziano. Cut each chevron in half to form 8 parallelograms. Ink cube with Burgundy ink and press point of parallelogram into corner of stamp to obtain a heart design in the same position on 4 pieces. • Mark the center of the Cream square with a light pencil. Glue or tape 1 stamped half-chevron so the tip points towards the top of the card. Arrange the other Pink parallelograms around the pencil point so they all touch, alternating stamped and plain Pink shapes. • Punch 2 chevrons from Fleur des Lis paper. Line up the punch so the pattern is the same on both. Cut each one in half and then in half again to make 8 triangles. Choose 4 triangles whose patterns match and glue to the tips of the unstamped Pink shapes. • Punch out 1 Burgundy chevron and cut into 4 triangles. Arrange and glue triangles into the corners of the Cream square. Embellish the corners with frosted stickers. • Punch out 1 large and 1 small flower from Burgundy and Fleur des Lis paper. Glue the smaller one on top of the larger one. Attach a frosted flower sticker on the top. • **Finish:** Adhere the quilted piece to center of card.

Black and Ivory Geometric Beaded Card

MATERIALS: *Papers by Catherine* Wrought Iron Indian Silk-screen (Gold/Black, Gold/Ivory) • Cardstock (Black, Ivory) • 9 Black 5 mm sequins • Seed beads (8 Black, 9 Pearl) • Gold stickers • Black and Ivory embroidery threads • Beading needle • Piercing tool • Paper clips • Tape • Glue stick

INSTRUCTIONS: **Card:** Cut cardstock 5½" x 8½". Fold in half (4¼" x 5½"). Cut Ivory cardstock 3¾" x 3¾". • **Embroidery:** Lay copy of beading pattern, shown on page 20, on Ivory cardstock, securing with paper clips. Pierce each outer dot and remove pattern. • Tape thread to back of Ivory cardstock. Stitch 1 motif. Add a Black sequin and Pearl seed bead in the center. Add a Black bead to the left of the motif. • Stitch the next motif, continuing until embroidery and beadwork is completed. • **Tea bag Folding:** Cut 4 each Black and Ivory Wrought Iron 1½" squares. • See folding diagram. Fold 1 Black and 1 Ivory tea bag medallion. • Glue Black tea bag medallion in the center of the embroidered motifs. Glue the Ivory medallion on top of the Black one. • Sew 1 Black sequin and 1 Pearl seed bead in the middle of the medallion through the Ivory cardstock. • **Finish:** Attach beaded Ivory cardstock to the front of the Black card. Add Gold border stickers around the edges of the Ivory cardstock. Add Gold stickers to top of card.

In the Wind Pattern

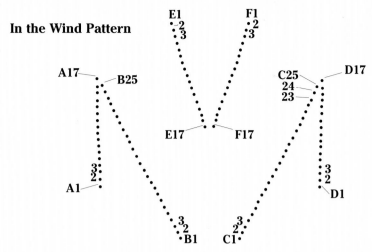

E1 F1
2 2
3 3

A17 B25

C25 D17
24
23

E17 F17

3 3
2 2
A1 D1

3 3
2 2
B1 C1

Piercing. Cut out or photocopy the desired pattern. Attach to open card with masking tape (that has been pressed against fabric to reduce stickiness and prevent damage to card). Place on piercing pad.

Pierce card with a fine tool holding tool vertically. Check the pattern against light for any unpierced holes. Remove pattern.

Embroidery. Select and cut 24"-36" of thread. Double thread for an attractive effect. Insert needle from back of card leaving a 1½" tail. Secure tail with tape outside the pierced holes. When ending thread, secure in the same manner.

Tip: Insert the needle in one hole at a time to prevent paper tears.

Finish. Glue coordinating cardstock on the back of design to hide stitching.

Tips:
• The needle should always be thinner than the piercing tool. Check by inserting needle in tool packaging or in a pierced hole.
• Dip end of thread in glue to prevent fraying. Allow thread to dry.

Star in My Heart Box Pattern and Just For You Card Pattern

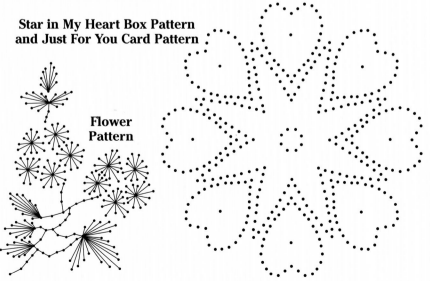

Flower Pattern

Paper, Paint Stamps, Tiles and Dragonflies

Dragonfly Luminaria

by Susan Pickering Rothamel

Dragonflies are such a popular motif, and these are particularly beautiful with their copper antennae. The glazed mica tiles soften the candlelight and make the dragonflies stand out in relief. Add a bit of romance to your patio table or sun room with this lovely centerpiece.

MATERIALS: Mulberry *Papers by Catherine* • Sandi Miller Art Stamps (Dragonfly) • *Pinata* (Inks, Claro Extender) • *US ArtQuest* (Gloss Perfect Paper Adhesive, Spray webbing, 4 mica 5" x 6" embossing tiles, Texture sponge) • Jacquard Lumiere (Halo Pink/Gold, Black) • Dragonfly shape • Cardboard tubes or dowels • Beads • *Artistic Wire* 24 gauge Copper wire • Paintbrush • Glue gun

INSTRUCTIONS: **Mulberry paper:** Spritz mulberry paper with Extender. While wet, drizzle Blue and Green inks. Sponge liberally to cover paper. Let dry.
• **Tiles**: On 2 tiles, sponge glossy medium over entire surface creating a water glass effect. Let dry. • On other 2 tiles, stamp dragonfly with Black paint. •
Dragonflies: Adhere 2 inked mulberry papers to the back of the stamped tile. On the remaining papers, draw 7 dragonflies and cut out. Adhere 1 dragonfly to each water glass tile. • Glue Copper wire to form antennae and tails to remaining 5 dragonflies. Adhere to stamped tiles. • **Luminaria**: Cut 4 sets of 3 different lengths of tubes or dowels. Paint with Pink/Gold. Also paint 4 large round beads for the feet and 12 smaller beads for the top of the tubes. Let dry. • Glue 3 different sizes of tubes together with hot glue. Glue a large bead to the bottom of the tubes as a foot and adhere a smaller bead to the tops of each of the 3 tubes. Assemble all 4 sets of legs. • Glue tiles to legs. • Place a lighted candle in center.

Paper Flower Vase

by Susan Pickering Rothamel

Dragonflies make another appearance in tin on this vase covered in decorative paper.

MATERIALS: Glass or plastic vase • *Papers by Catherine* (Indian Cotton paper) • Craft paper • *Jacquard* Lumiere (Halo Pink/Gold, Halo Violet/Gold, Halo Blue/Green, Pearlescent Turquoise) • Black *Krylon* spray webbing • *US ArtQuest* (Matte Perfect Paper Adhesive, Tinz Ivy and Dragonfly, Great Tape) • Wood block beads • Black acrylic paint • Paintbrush

INSTRUCTIONS: **Pattern**: Wrap craft paper around vase, forming the pattern for the desired height and shape of the finished piece. • Transfer pattern to Cotton paper. Cut or tear edges. Brush thin coats of 3-4 different colors of metallic paints, blending the edges well. Cover entirely. Let dry. • Lightly spray with webbing. • **Vase**: Wrap paper around vase. Use tape liberally to hold the form. Grommets, wire, and brads may also be used. • Tear any extra paper into 1" strips. Adhere to vase in a diagonal direction. • **Base**: Paint 4 wood blocks Black. Attach to the bottom of the vase. • **Decorations**: Paint tin dragonflies and ivy with acrylic paint. Adhere them to the vase.

Quilted Cards
by Catherine Mace

Making Quilted Cards is easy and fun with so many punches and beautiful papers to choose from!

Black Gold 4-Square Card

MATERIALS: *Papers by Catherine* (Gold Bamboo) • Cardstock (Cream, Black) • *Emagination Crafts* Punch (large chevron, teardrop, 1⅝" square) • *Stamp in the Hand* Ornate Pattern stamp • *Ancient Page* Black ink • Craft knife • Metal edge ruler • Cutting mat • Double-sided tape • White glue
INSTRUCTIONS: **Stamp:** Cut a 5½" square of Cream cardstock. Stamp the Ornate Pattern with Black ink. Let dry. • **Card:** Cut Cream cardstock 5½" x 11". Fold into a 5½" square • Cut 4 strips of stamped paper ¼" x 5½". Glue to edges of card to make a border. • **Pattern:** Cut 4 Black 2" squares. Glue to card. • Punch 4 squares from Gold bamboo paper. Tape to card. • Punch 4 chevron shapes from stamped cardstock. Punch 3 teardrops in each one. Glue stamped chevrons on top of the Gold paper, each one offset from the edge slightly, to show a Black border.

Red/Gold/Black Harlequin Card

MATERIALS: *Papers by Catherine* Tiziano (Black, Honey Gold, Red) • *Emagination Crafts* Large chevron punch • *Stampendous* Class-A-Peels Silver marquis stickers • Double-sided tape
INSTRUCTIONS: **Card:** Cut Black paper 5½" x 8½". Fold in half (4¼" x 5½"). • **Chevrons:** Punch 4 Gold chevrons and 4 Red chevrons. See Pattern construction diagram. • **Finish:** Glue pattern to card. Add Silver stickers.

Blue Delft Tile Card

MATERIALS: White cardstock • *Papers by Catherine* (Red/Gold/White Floral Yuzen, Red Tiziano) • *Impression Obsession* Delft Cube #3 • Cobalt Blue ink • Craft knife • Foam squares • *Yasutomo* Gold Metallic marker • Double-sided tape • Foam tape • Glue stick
INSTRUCTIONS: **Card:** Cut White cardstock 5" x 9". Fold in half (4½" x 5"). Ink edges of card with Gold pen. • **Delft Background:** Cut White cardstock 4¼" x 4¾". Stamp tile in Cobalt ink. • Cut Floral paper into ½" wide strips. Glue strips to card. • **Center:** Cut a 2" square of Red Tiziano. Glue to center of card. • Cut 2 White 1½" squares. Stamp tile with Cobalt ink. Cut out one tile on border. Trim edges with Gold pen. On remaining tile, cut out interior design with craft knife. Stack and adhere tiles to card with foam tape.

Strip Quilting with Paper
by Catherine Mace

Harlequin Card Construction Diagrams

1. Punch out pieces.

2. Tape ends together. Note: Ted on top on left, Yellow on top at right.

3. Cut down middle.

4. Tape pattern together.

Tan Swirls Card

MATERIALS: *Papers by Catherine* (Fern Swirls Yuzen, Tan Swirls Yuzen, Green/Red/Black Yuzen, Red Tiziano) • White cardstock • Bone folder • Double-sided tape • Glue stick

INSTRUCTIONS: **Card:** Cut White cardstock 6½" x 9½". Fold in half (4¾" x 6½"). Cut Red Tiziano paper 4½" x 6¼". Glue to card. • **Pattern:** Cut 4 White rectangles 2⅛" x 3". Cut decorative papers into strips ½" x 4". Arrange and glue strips to White rectangles as shown. Use the flat edge of a bone folder to smooth out the paper. Trim off all excess paper from all edges. • **Finish:** Arrange rectangles on card. See photo. Some of the rectangles must be turned upside down. Tape rectangles to card.

Black Maple Leaf Card

MATERIALS: *Papers by Catherine* (Black Tiziano, Gold Glossy, Maple Leaf Yuzen) • Punches (Medium heart, Small flower) • *Stampendous* Class-A-Peels translucent frosted stickers • White glue • Double-sided tape • Glue stick

INSTRUCTIONS: **Card:** Cut Black paper 4¾" x 9½". Fold to make a 4¾" square. Cut Gold paper into a 4½" square. Glue to card. • **Pattern:** Cut 4 Black 2" squares. Adhere to card. • Cut ½" wide strips of Maple Leaf paper. Glue Maple Leaf strip diagonally across each Black square. • Punch 4 hearts of Maple Leaf paper. If Maple Leaf paper is too light for the punch, back it with a sheet of copy paper. Glue a heart shape in the corner of each Black square. • Punch a small flower from Black paper. Add a daisy sticker. Put a drop of White glue on the back of the small flower and in the center of the quilted card. Allow to dry 30 minutes, then stick together.

Florentine and Calligraphy Card

MATERIALS: *Papers by Catherine* (Red Florentine Italian print, Italian Calligraphy, Light Green Tiziano, Honey Gold Tiziano) • Cardstock (White, Navy Blue) • Double-sided tape • Glue stick

INSTRUCTIONS: **Card:** Cut Navy Blue cardstock 6¼" x 11". Fold to 5½" x 6¼". • **Mats:** Cut, stack and glue the following mats to the card: Honey Gold 5¼" x 5¾"; Light Green 5" x 5½". • **Pattern:** Cut 4 White rectangles, 2¼" x 2½". Cut Florentine paper into ¾" wide strips. Cut Calligraphy paper into ½" wide strips. Adhere Florentine paper diagonally across each White square. Adhere Calligraphy paper on each side. Arrange panels. Adhere to card.

Lovely Paper Mosaics
by Lisa Larsen

Basic Technique

MATERIALS: Decorative *Papers by Catherine* • Sticky paper • Embossing powder • Embossing pen • Heat gun • Cardstock • Rubber Stamps • Ink
INSTRUCTIONS: Cut strips of pastel papers varying the widths from ¼" to ¾". • Adhere strips to sticky paper leaving a ⅛" gap between the strips. • Cut strips perpendicular to strip lengths in varying widths ¼" to ¾". • Adhere new strips to another sticky paper, again leaving a ⅛" gap between the strips. These strips may be staggered to achieve a random effect. • Dip piece into embossing powder. Allow powder to adhere to sticky paper surface. Shake off excess powder. Heat until powder is melted. • Cut piece to desired size. • Run an embossing pen or pad along the edges of the mosaic piece, and emboss.

Asian Peony Mosaic Card

MATERIALS: *Papers by Catherine* (Black/Gold Scallop Yuzen; Fawn Cranes Yuzen) • 2 Gold eyelets • Twig • 2 sheets sticky paper 4¼" x 5⅝" • Black cardstock • *Ink-N-Rubber Expressions, LLC* stamps (Asian Peony, Love) • Black pigment ink • Gold Detail embossing powder • *Krylon* Gold leafing pen • Gold *Mizuhiki* Cord • Glue
INSTRUCTIONS: **Card:** Cut Black cardstock 7" x 10". Fold in half (5" x 7"). Edge card with Gold pen. • **Mosaic:** Follow Basic Technique instructions to make a 4¼" x 5⅝" mosaic piece. Set 2 eyelets in the top of the finished mosaic. • **Stamps:** Stamp two Asian Peony squares and an Asian Love image on Black cardstock with pigment ink. Emboss with Gold. Cut out stamped images and trim squares with Gold pen. Glue stamped pieces on paper mosaic. • **Twig:** Hang the paper mosaic from the stick with Gold Mizuhiki cord, and coil remaining cord around the stick as a decorative accent. Glue stick and mosaic piece to card.

Rose Bunch Mosaic Card

MATERIALS: Pastel handmade Bamboo impression papers (Lilac, Pink, Light Green, Lavender); White watercolor paper • 4 Silver brads • 2 sheets sticky paper 4½" x 5½" • *Ink-N-Rubber Expressions, LLC* Rose Bunch stamp • *Posh Impressions* "Love is in the Air" stamp • Brown *Memories* ink • Lilac opaque embossing powder • Glue stick
INSTRUCTIONS: **Card:** Cut Pink paper 7" x 9¾" Fold in half (4⅞" x 7"). Cut Lavender paper 4⅞" x 3½". Adhere Lavender paper to card front. • **Mosaic:** Follow Basic Technique instructions to make a 4¼" x 5¼" mosaic. Attach to card with brads. • **Rose:** Stamp Rose Bunch in Brown ink. Color as desired. • Emboss edges with Lilac powder by swiping the edge of the card with embossing ink, dipping into Lilac powder, then heating with heat tool. Adhere to card. • **Title:** Cut White paper 1½" x 2¾". Stamp and emboss words in Lilac on White paper. • Cut Lilac mat 1¾" x 3". Glue title together. Glue to card.

1. Position strips ⅛" apart on sticky paper.

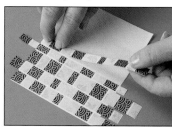

2. Cut strips apart.

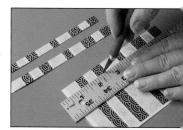

3. Position strips ⅛" apart on a new sheet of sticky paper.

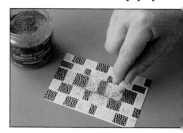

4. Add embossing powder.

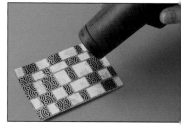

5. Heat until powder melts.

Italian Key Tile Card

Shown on page 26

MATERIALS:
Papers by Catherine (Italian Blue Tile) • Cardstock (Navy Blue, White) • Silver Tassel • 2 sheets sticky paper 4¼" x 5½" • Silver embossing powder • Blue Pigment Ink • Clear detail embossing powder • Hole punch • Glue

INSTRUCTIONS:
Card: Cut Navy Blue cardstock 5½" x 8½". Fold in half (4¼" x 5½"). • Mosaic: Follow Basic Technique instructions for mosaic. Trim piece to 4" x 5¼". Adhere to card. • Key: Stamp Key onto White cardstock with Blue pigment ink. Emboss with clear powder. Trim the piece to fit between mosaic tiles. Edge stamped piece with Blue ink. Punch hole at the top of the key and thread a silver tassel through it. Glue to card.

Indulge in some creative Paper Play

Paper Butterfly Mobile

by Catherine Mace

Butterfly Mobile

This lovely mobile would be at home anywhere butterflies and nature are appreciated. The folded butterflies also make beautiful decorations for handmade greeting cards.

MATERIALS: Papers by Catherine (24 Assorted 4" square Japanese Yuzen papers) • 8" grapevine wreath • Scrap paper • Assorted beads • Large-holed bead • 9 Gold 1½" head pins • 10 Gold 1½" eye pins • Clear shrink plastic • Craf-T Decorating Chalk • Floral rubber stamps • White ink • Yasutomo Gold Metallic marker • Wooden clothespin • Hole punch •Jewelry snips • Jewelry pliers • Heat tool • Black thread • 72" monofilament thread • Gloss acrylic medium • Paintbrush • Needle or awl • Fine grit sandpaper • White clear drying craft glue • Glue stick

INSTRUCTIONS: **Butterfly**: Use glue stick to adhere wrong sides of Washi together. Paint edges of paper with Gold pen. While paper is still damp with adhesive, follow folding diagrams (on page 28) to make butterfly. Apply a small dot of glue under wings, inside the body, and inside the head fold. Fold a strip of scrap paper several times, wrap front of butterfly head with paper to protect Washi, and secure with clothespin until glue sets. Remove clothespin and allow to completely dry. Paint butterfly with at least 2 coats of acrylic medium. When dry, press down firmly on butterfly head, to flatten the pointy part of the head. Use awl or heavy needle to poke a hole in butterfly head, straight through body. Thread 1 seed bead, 1 small round bead, and 1 seed bead on head pin; insert through butterfly body, from bottom to top. Slide on matching beads on shaft of head pin that protrudes through body; use pliers to form a closed loop to keep beads from falling off. Make 12 beaded

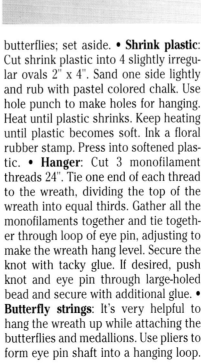

butterflies; set aside. • **Shrink plastic**: Cut shrink plastic into 4 slightly irregular ovals 2" x 4". Sand one side lightly and rub with pastel colored chalk. Use hole punch to make holes for hanging. Heat until plastic shrinks. Keep heating until plastic becomes soft. Ink a floral rubber stamp. Press into softened plastic. • **Hanger**: Cut 3 monofilament threads 24". Tie one end of each thread to the wreath, dividing the top of the wreath into equal thirds. Gather all the monofilaments together and tie together through loop of eye pin, adjusting to make the wreath hang level. Secure the knot with tacky glue. If desired, push knot and eye pin through large-holed bead and secure with additional glue. • **Butterfly strings**: It's very helpful to hang the wreath up while attaching the butterflies and medallions. Use pliers to form eye pin shaft into a hanging loop.

• Cut Black thread into 9 lengths 24". Use pliers to bend eye pin in half, forming a hook. Tie one end of Black thread to loop in eye pin, knotting twice and securing with a drop of glue. Cut off excess thread. Arrange threaded "hooks" around the bottom edge of the wreath, leaving the hook open until the placement is satisfactory. Thread loose end of thread through closed loop above butterfly. Tie a single knot so butterfly can be moved up and down the thread later, if necessary. Farther down the thread, tie another butterfly or a shrink plastic medallion. Make a double knot with last item tied on, and add a drop of glue to secure all knots. Trim off excess threads and close all hooks. Trim excess wire from eye pins with jewelry snips to complete mobile.

Continued on page 28

Requires 4-6" square of paper .

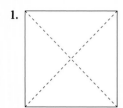

1.

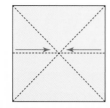

1. Wrong side up, fold and unfold paper like this. Turn paper over, fold in half horizontally. Unfold. Push in sides with horizontal folds.

2. Bring tip of folded triangle up to loose edges and crease well.

2.

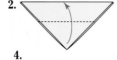

3.

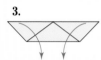

4.

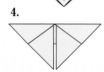

3 & 4. On both sides of new smaller triangle (which will become the head) you will see 2 layers of paper, one on top of the other. These layers are also shaped like triangles and will become the butterfly's wings. Fold down the left top layer, so that its top edge lines up with the center of the head triangle. Crease well, repeat on right. This will result in the basic butterfly shape.

5.

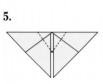

Pinch triangle area together to form head and body.

5. Fold butterfly in half so back of wings touch each other. His body is the thick part in the middle. To give it shape (which is also a triangle) pinch the head of the folded in half body with thumb and forefinger and splay the wings out on the table. One wing goes to the left and one wing spreads out to the right. Visualize a triangle that will make the body: the wide part of the triangle is at the head and it tapers off at the end of the body which lies between the 2 lower wings. Fold the thick paper first in one direction and then the other along this imaginary line. Add a drop of white glue to the bottom of the butterfly to make it hold its shape. The size of the height of the head varies with the size of the square of paper being folded. When a 4" square of paper is used the head is about 1/4" height.

6.

6. To finish butterfly fold each wing tip in along the open edges about 3/8" then unfold making sure the crease is sharp. Open up paper and make a "reverse fold" : push the pointy tip of the wing inside itself so it becomes squared off. Repeat this with all the wings.

7.

7. Add a drop of glue anywhere the butterfly body seems to be unfolding but do not glue the open edges of the wings shut.

Ballerina Photo Album
by Beverly Montez and Catherine Mace

These albums stand up on a desk or table. One stores a baby announcement while the other keeps several photos on hand. The diagrams provided make it easy for you to assemble these fun projects.

MATERIALS: *Papers by Catherine* (Black Accordion Fold Card 5" x 25", Coral Cranes Yuzen) • Matboards (Three 6" x 6", Two 1" x 6") • Heavy Cardstock (5½" x 5½") • 20 Transparent Photo Corners • Craft knife • *Tombow* glue stick

INSTRUCTIONS: Cut Coral paper into these pieces: A- 8" x 23", B- 5½" x 15¾", C- 6½" x 6½". • Cut a 3½" x 3½" window in the first 6" x 6" board. • Arrange boards on Coral paper "A" as shown in diagram. Cover all boards with paper "A". Cut the window in the first board by slicing diagonally from each inside corner to center of opening. Fold flaps around inside edges. Trim as needed. Glue down. • Cover boards 2 - 5 with Coral paper "B". • Cover cardstock with Coral paper "C". Glue "C" behind the opening in board #1, leaving the edge next to board #2 unglued to allow insertion of photo. • Attach photos to accordion pages with photo corners. Glue to outside of board #5. • Fold boards as shown to make frame stand up.

Ballerina Photo Album Diagrams

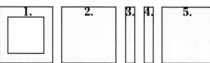

1. Cut boards.

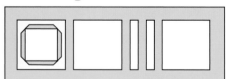

4. Your paper will look like this.

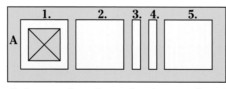

2. Arrange boards on Coral paper. Leave 3/8" between boards 1 & 2 and 1/4" between other boards. Cut window.

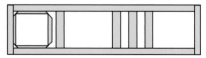

5. Fold down top and bottom flaps of paper A. Glue. Fold ends toward center and glue.

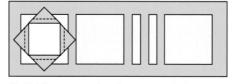

3. Fold paper to back, trim and glue.

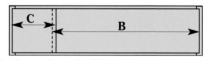

6. Cover boards 2-5 with coral paper B. Cover cardstock with Coral paper C. Glue C behind opening in board #1.

Beautiful
Papers
Make
Easy
Projects
Special

Baby Photo Announcement

by Catherine Mace

MATERIALS: *Papers by Catherine* (Rossi Italian Floral Print) • Matboards (Three 5" x 7", Two 1½" x 7") • Heavy cardstock 4½" x 6¼" • Ivory notecard: 4½" x 6¼"

INSTRUCTIONS: Cut Floral paper into three pieces: A- 9" x 22", B- 6½" x 15½", C- 5½" x 7½". • See Board diagram. Cut a 3" x 4½" window in the first 5" x 7" board. • See Assembly Diagrams. Leaving a ¼" space between boards, arrange boards on Floral paper "A" as shown. Glue paper to all boards. Cut the window in the first board by slicing diagonally from each inside corner to center of opening. Fold flaps around inside edges. Trim as needed. Glue flaps down. • Cover boards 2 - 5 with Floral paper "B". • Cover cardstock with Floral paper "C". Glue "C" behind the opening in board #1, leaving the edge next to board #2 unglued to allow insertion of photo. • Computer print information on notecard and glue to outside of board #5. • Fold boards as shown to make frame stand up.

Frame Stand for Photo Album and Baby Announcement

This end view shows how the boards are folded to make the frames stand up.

Baby Photo Announcement Diagram

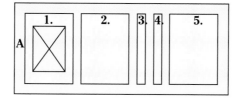

1. Cut boards. Arrange boards on Floral paper A. Leave ¹/₄" between boards. Cut out window.

2. Follow Ballerina Photo Album Diagrams on page 28, steps 3-5 to assemble announcement. Replace Coral paper with Floral paper.

Les Petites Fleurs with Punches
by Catherine Mace

Making Les Petites Fleurs

GENERAL MATERIALS: Ultra-fine crystal glitter • Shaping tool or embossing stylus • Dense foam mat or mouse pad for shaping flowers • Tweezers • Needle tool, toothpick, or skewer for curling petals and leaves • Scissors • Craft knife • White, clear drying, craft glue

INSTRUCTIONS: **Basket Card:** Cut cardstock 4" x 5". Fold in half (2½" x 4"). Trace Basket Card pattern onto front of card, placing the edge of the basket on the side fold of the card. Cut out the basket. Set aside. • **Flower shaping**: Place each flower on mat and use a round-headed tool, such as embossing stylus, to press down in a circular manner in the center of each flower. This will make the leaves curl upwards.

1. Use an embossing tool and foam mat to shape flowers.

Framed Wreath

MATERIALS: *Papers by Catherine* (Indian Silk-screen Red/Gold Trellis; Light Green, Moss Green and Honey Gold Tiziano, White cardstock with Silk fibers) • Wood frame with glass • Markers (Yellow, Green) • Pencil • Scrap paper • *EK Success* punches (daisy, grass, small circle, flower, lotus)

INSTRUCTIONS: **Background:** Cut a White square to fit your frame, draw a circle in the center. • **Leaves**: Punch grass shapes from Moss Green and Light Green Tiziano. • **Flowers**: Punch lotus and daisy shapes from Red/Gold. Shape. See general instructions. Place a drop of glue in the center of each lotus and drop in shaped daisy flower. Let dry. • Punch daisies from Honey Gold Tiziano. Use a Yellow marker to color around petals, allowing color of paper to show through in petal center. Bend every other petal backwards over needle tool or awl.

It's just like arranging real flowers, but you won't sneeze!

Shape the center, causing the flower to cup upwards with half of the petals bending backwards for realism. • Punch small flowers from Yellow Tiziano, shape. Dot center with Yellow marker in the flower center. Color Yellow Tiziano with Yellow marker, punch out small circles. Glue in center of larger flowers. • **Assembly**: Run a bead of glue on the pencil line. Arrange the leaves on the ring of glue. Use tweezers to dip bottom of shaped flowers into glue and place on the wreath. Use enough glue to lift the flowers up off the wreath base. Let dry. • If needed, add more leaves in both shades of Green to fill the empty areas. When completely dry, place under glass in a frame.

Framed Bluebells

MATERIALS: *Papers by Catherine* (Vellum, Yellow Vellum, Green Metallic, Light Green Tiziano) • Black cardstock • *EK Success* daisy punch • *Tsukineko Brilliance* Sky Blue pigment ink • Wood frame with glass

INSTRUCTIONS: **Background:** Cut Black cardstock to fit frame. **Flowers**: Drag Sky Blue pigment pad over clear vellum to tint. Let dry. Punch out daisies. Score the center of each flower petal to the point at which the petal is attached to the flower center. Roll the tip of the petal back over a toothpick. Shape flower. See general instructions. Press on flower center until petals curl upwards to form a bluebell tube. **Stems**: Fold strips of Green metallic paper and use scissors to cut 1/16" away from fold through both thicknesses. The paper will curl slightly for a natural look. • From folded Green Tiziano and Green metallic paper cut leaves of different lengths and widths. **Stamens:** Cut Yellow vellum into rectangle ¼" x ½", and fringe one side with at 6-8 slits. Wind the uncut portion of this rectangle around a toothpick. Flare out the strands. Glue to the center of the bluebell. Not all flowers need stamens. See photo. **Assembly**: Use tweezers to dip bottoms of completed bluebells into glue, then attach to flower stems. Use 6 bluebells for the longer stems and 5 for the shorter ones. Glue to cardstock. When completely dry, place under glass in a frame.

You can make delicate and beautiful floral gift cards and framed artwork easily, using simple paper punches and high quality paper.

. Glue flower center to daisy.   3. Glue flowers to wreath.

Red Poinsettias

MATERIALS: *Papers by Catherine* (Frost Pearlescent, Red and Green metal-
ic paper) • Textured Sage cardstock • 5 Yellow glass seed beads • *EKSuccess*
unches (daisy, flower, ⅛" circle) • Yellow marker
INSTRUCTIONS: **Card**: Make Sage basket card. See general instructions.
Flowers: Punch 16 Red and 8 Blue Green daisies. Shape each daisy. See
eneral instructions. Put drop of glue on 8 Red shaped daisies with tooth-
ick and use tweezers to place second set of Red shaped daisy petals on top
f first, offsetting top flower slightly, so both layers of petals show. • Put a
rop of glue in the center of each Blue Green daisy and attach Red petals,
gain turning petals so they do not line up with each other. Use a Yellow
arker to color the Tiziano paper. Punch ⅛" circles and glue to center of
owers. Dab each Yellow poinsettia flower center with glue. Sprinkle with
litter. Add streaks of glue to a few Red petals and sprinkle with glitter. Let
ry. • Punch 5 small flowers from Frost Pearlescent paper and shape on mat.
lace a good-size drop of glue in center of each flower and drop in Yellow
eed bead. Glue will dry clear, so use plenty. • **Assembly**: Arrange poinset-
as around basket and handle. Add tiny white flowers with seed bead cen-
rs where appropriate. Glue in place.

Gladiolas

MATERIALS: *Papers by Catherine*
Light Green, Moss Green and Honey
old Tiziano) • Ivory cardstock •
Markers (Yellow, Green) • *EKSuccess*
mall flower punches
INSTRUCTIONS: **Card**: Cut Ivory
ardstock 4" x 5". Fold in half (2½" x 4").
dge card with Green marker. • **Flowers**:
unch out 17 Honey Gold flowers. Go
round edge of each one with Yellow
arker. Shape. See general instructions.
Leaves: Fold a small piece of Green
iziano in half. Use scissors to cut a long
ear shape, with crease down the cen-
r. This will become a leaf. Cut several of
ese, some of them very thin so that
ey curl. Cut from both shades of Green
aper. Wind some of the very thin ones,
ill folded, around a needle to make
em spiral and coil. Leave others as
ey are. • **Assembly**: Glue leaves to
ont of card. Glue flowers to leaf spears.
mbellish with curled tendrils.

**Basket Pattern
for
Red Poinsettias
and
Flowers and Vines**

Flowers and Vines Basket

MATERIALS: *Papers by Catherine* (Amethyst, Plum and Red Metallic; Light Green, Moss Green and
Honey Gold Tiziano) • Cardstock scrap • 6 transparent Peach seed beads • *EKSuccess* punches (3-
flower corner, small flower, vine) • Green water-based marker • Green ink • Sponge
INSTRUCTIONS: **Card**: Make basket card with Yellow Tiziano paper following general instructions.
• Punch vine design at random from scrap cardstock to make a template. Sponge Green ink over template to make vine design on card front. • **Flowers**: Punch flowers from Amethyst and Plum papers
with 3-flower punch. Shape each flower. See general instructions. • Layer a small shaped flower onto
the larger flower shape. Alternate colors, if desired. Punch out Honey Gold flower centers. Glue to
Amethyst flower centers. Add glue and glitter to Honey Gold flower centers. • Punch small flowers
from Plum paper. Shape and glue seed beads to the center of each one. Let dry. • **Vine**: Lightly color
some of the Green paper with marker. Punch out Vines, so colors are varied. • **Assembly**: Arrange
vines on basket handle and glue in place. Glue flowers in place.

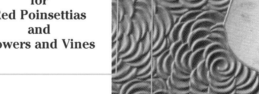

Curled Flower Patterns

Photo and Instructions are on pages 34 & 35.

Curled Metallic Papers for Cards

by Babette Cox

Brass Bow Card

MATERIALS: *Papers by Catherine* (Gold Metalli Silver Metallic; Indian Silk-screen Gold/Ochre Iv Vines, Gold/Purple Ivy Vines, Purple/Silver Flora Fern Tone on Tone Swirls Yuzen) • Black cardstoc • Brass bow charm • Mini brads • Green ink pad *Postmodern Design* GL2-101-F Tribal Cube stamp Craft knife • Paper punches • Cutting board Metal-edged ruler • Bamboo skewer • Gel Supe Glue • 1/8" double-sided tape

INSTRUCTIONS: **Rolled paper**: Cut Ochre Iv Vines, Purple Floral, Fern, and Yuzen papers 4" x 5 • Stamp bars from Tribal Cube on back of th Purple Floral. • Put 1/8" double-sided tape on th front of the pages on all 4 sides very close to th edges. Tape papers together, pattern down, as fo lows: Ivy Vines, Yuzen, Swirls, Purple Floral. Th stamped side of the Purple Floral will be on top. D not remove cover of tape from the stamped shee • Using cutting board and craft knife, cut an "X diagonally from corner to corner leaving 1/4" unc at each corner. • Curl each layer back with a skew er. • **Card base**: Cut Black cardstock 6" x 12". Fol card in half. Cut Purple Ivy Vines 5 7/8" x 5 7/8". Tap to card. • Cut Silver Metallic 5 3/4" x 5 3/4". Tape t card. • **Top**: Cut Gold Metallic 5 1/4" x 5 1/4". Cut a wi dow in the top portion 3 1/2" x 4 1/2". Position windo over the curled edges. Tape stack to the back of th window. • Thin papers are easier to punch whe lined with a single sheet of typing paper. Punc flowers from Swirls, Yuzen, and Purple Ivy paper Stack flowers and adhere to Gold paper with brad Tape Gold paper to card. • Glue the brass bo charm in place.

Copper Face Card

MATERIALS: *Papers by Catherine* (Copper, Plu and Blue Green Metallic; Indian Silk-scree Gold/Ivory Wrought Iron) • Black cardstock • Cla polymer face • Craft knife • Cutting board • Meta edged ruler • Bamboo skewer • Gel Super Glue 1/8" double-sided tape

INSTRUCTIONS: **Rolled paper**: Cut Metall papers 4" x 4". • Put 1/8" double-sided tape on th front of the pages on all 4 sides very close to th edges. Tape papers together as follows: Plun Copper, Blue Green. Do not remove cover of tap from the top sheet. • Using cutting board and cra knife, cut an "X" diagonally from corner to corn leaving 1/4" uncut at each corner. • Curl each lay back with a skewer. • **Card base**: Cut Black car stock 6" x 12". Fold card in half. Cut Plum Metall 5 7/8" x 5 7/8". Tape to card. • Cut Wrought Iron pap 5 5/8" x 5 5/8". Tape to card. • Tape rolled paper i place. Adhere clay face.

Indulge your creative spirit with exquisite papers in bold metallics and intricate prints. Rolled papers are easy to make. Once you start, you will find many applications for this dimensional embellishment on cards, wall art and scrapbook pages.

1. Apply double-sided tape to edges.

2. Stack papers.

3. Cut an "X" 1/4" from the corners.

4. Curl the edges of the papers.

5. Position the foil window over curled pieces.

I would like to extend a heart-felt thanks to the designers who helped make this book possible.
- Catherine Mace

ToniAnn "TA" Carbone

Lea Cioci

Babette Cox

Edie Hedman

Lisa Larsen

Beverly Montez

Susan Pickering Rothamel

Linda Standart

Lin Stanley